W9-BXT-433

Tell Me Why

WHY?

Bears Hibernate

Susan H. Gray

Published in the United States of America by Cherry Lake Publishing
Ann Arbor, Michigan
www.cherrylakepublishing.com

Consultants: Dr. Stephen S. Ditchkoff, Professor of Wildlife Sciences, Auburn University,
Auburn, Alabama
Reading Adviser: Marla Conn, Readability, Inc.

Photo Credits: © PathDoc/Shutterstock Images, cover, 1, 7; © michaeljung/Shutterstock Images, cover, 1,
21; © xavier gallego morell/Shutterstock Images, cover, 1, 15; © Joe Mercier/Shutterstock Images, cover, 1;
© Eduard Kyslynskyy/Shutterstock Images, cover, 1; © Wolfgang Kruck /Shutterstock Images, cover, 1;
© CoolR/Shutterstock Images, 5; © BGSmith/Shutterstock Images, 7; © Erik Mandre/Shutterstock
Images, 9; © Mighty Sequoia Studio/Shutterstock Images, 11; © l i g h t p o e t/Shutterstock Images, 13;
© © Angelaforker | Dreamstime.com - Home For A Bear Photo, 15; © Aspen Photo/Shutterstock Images,
17; © Hung Chung Chih/Shutterstock Images, 19; © PhotonCatcher/Shutterstock Images, 21

Library of Congress Cataloging-in-Publication Data

Gray, Susan Heinrichs, author.
 Bears hibernate / by Susan H. Gray.
    pages cm. -- (Tell me why)
 Summary: "Young children are naturally curious about animals. Tell Me Why Bears
Hibernate offers answers to their most compelling questions about why bears
sleep all winter. Age-appropriate explanations and appealing photos
encourage readers to continue their quest for knowledge. Additional text
features and search tools, including a glossary and an index, help students
locate information and learn new words."—Provided by publisher.
 Audience: Ages 6-10
 Audience: K to grade 3.
 Includes bibliographical references and index.
 ISBN 978-1-63188-990-5 (hardcover) -- ISBN 978-1-63362-029-2 (pbk.) --
ISBN 978-1-63362-068-1 (pdf) -- ISBN 978-1-63362-107-7 (ebook) 1.
Bears--Hibernation--Juvenile literature. 2. Bears--Wintering--Juvenile
literature. 3. Adaptation (Biology)--Juvenile literature. 4. Children's
questions and answers. I. Title.

QL737.C27G735 2015
599.78'1565--dc23
                                    2014031839

Cherry Lake Publishing would like to acknowledge the work of The Partnership for 21st Century Skills.
Please visit *www.p21.org* for more information.

Printed in the United States of America
Corporate Graphics

Table of Contents

Where Are the Bears?

Shawn and his family were visiting a state park. Spring had not yet arrived. So the weather was still very cool.

At the park, a ranger talked about the animals living there. Chipmunks would not be out yet. Some birds were still down south where it was warmer. Bears were **hibernating**. They would be hidden for 2 more months.

Many bears hibernate through the cold winter months.

Shawn thought of the TV shows he'd seen about bears. Some caught fish. Some sat and ate berries. He did not know that bears stayed hidden for months.

"Why are they hibernating?" Shawn asked.

The ranger turned to look at Shawn. "There is not enough food for bears right now," she explained. "But soon, food will be everywhere. Then they will leave their **dens**."

ASK QUESTIONS!

Talk to your family members. See if anyone knows why bears hibernate.

Bears feed on spring plants.

Lots and Lots of Food

"Many bears live in forests," the ranger said. "Pandas live in **bamboo** forests. They munch on bamboo leaves and stems. Brown bears also live in forests. They eat plants, berries, and insects.

"Some bears live in warm **swampy** areas," she continued. "Others live where it is very cold. Bears live in all sorts of places. But wherever they live, there must be plenty of food."

Bears are found all over the world.

The ranger went on. "Sometimes, bears eat other animals. But they also eat plants. They eat roots, fruit, berries, and nuts."

Shawn began thinking. Bears are huge animals. They must need lots of food. Then he looked around. It was still winter. The trees had no leaves. The grass looked dead. There were no berries anywhere. There was nothing for bears to eat.

Bears find a lot of food to eat in warmer months.

Bedtime!

The ranger interrupted Shawn's thoughts. She began to explain where all the bears were. "During the summer and fall, the bears ate and ate. They gained a lot of weight. The fat built up in their bodies. Their fur also grew thicker. As it got colder, they could not find enough food. It was time for them to hibernate."

Bears gain weight before hibernating.

In time, every bear withdrew into a den. The den is a hollowed-out place. It might be in a cave or on a hillside. It might be under a rock ledge. The den is not much larger than the bear. It is a tight space with little room.

The bear doesn't mind, though. He puts his furry back to the den's opening. He curls up in a big ball and shuts his eyes. Then something amazing happens.

This bear den is under a fallen tree.

The bear's breathing slows way down. His heartbeat slows down, too. The bear falls into a deep resting state. For the next few months, he does not leave the den. He won't even go to the bathroom. He will not eat a thing. His body will slowly use up the stored fat.

When warm weather returns, the bear opens his eyes. He stretches and sniffs the air. Now, food is everywhere. It's time to get out and eat!

Bears eat many kinds of food, including berries.

Not Everyone Hibernates

Not all bears hibernate. For example, pandas do not. They may run out of bamboo to eat. But then they just move to where there's more bamboo.

Black bears are another case. These bears live in Alaska, where it gets very cold. They also live in Florida, where it stays warm. The Alaska bears hibernate during the coldest months. But the Florida bears stay active all year.

Panda bears do not hibernate.

Bears are not the only animals that hibernate. Many bats, chipmunks, and mice also do. They all hibernate for the same reason. There's not much food in the **environment**.

Zoo workers can tell you more about hibernating animals. Rangers at state parks can, too. Rangers might even know where some animals' dens are. But do not try to find them. You don't want to bother a sleepy, hungry bear!

MAKE A GUESS!

This sun bear lives where trees are green all year long. Do you think it hibernates?

This sun bear lives in a warm place.

Think About It

If a hibernating bear is disturbed, it takes him a few minutes to wake up. Why is that?

Polar bears are hunters and eat mostly meat. They can find food all year long. Do you think they hibernate?

At what time of year is a hibernating bear's weight the highest?

Glossary

bamboo (bam-BOO) a fast-growing grass that has a tall, woody stem

dens (DENZ) the shelters of wild animals

environment (en-VY-run-munt) surroundings

hibernating (HY-bur-nay-teeng) spending the winter in a deep, restful state

swampy (SWOM-pee) like an area with wet, mushy ground

Find Out More

Books:

Kolpin, Molly. *Grizzly Bears*. North Mankato, MN: First Facts, 2011.

Kosara, Tori. *Hibernation*. Danbury, CT: Scholastic Paperbacks, 2012.

Nelson, Robin. *Hibernation*. Minneapolis: Lerner Classroom, 2010.

Web Sites:

The American Bear Association—Cubs Corner for Kids
www.americanbear.org/Kids%27%20questions.htm
Visit this site filled with questions and answers about bears, including information about their food and hibernation.

Idaho Public Television—Bears
http://idahoptv.org/dialogue4kids/archive/topicPage.cfm?topicID=1067
This site includes all sorts of audio and video programs about bears.

San Diego Zoo Kids
http://kids.sandiegozoo.org/animals/mammals/polar-bear
This page is all about polar bears, with basic information and links to photos, videos, and a live polar bear cam.

Index

About the Author

Susan H. Gray has a master's degree in zoology. She has worked in research and has taught college-level science classes. Susan has also written more than 140 science and reference books, but especially likes to write about animals. She and her husband, Michael, live in Cabot, Arkansas, with many pets.